T0208890

SCIENCE
▬ IN THE ▬
PULPIT

Jerry L. Artrip

iUniverse, Inc.

New York   Bloomington

SCIENCE IN THE PULPIT

iUniverse books may be ordered through booksellers or by contacting:

iUniverse
1663 Liberty Drive
Bloomington, IN 47403
www.iuniverse.com
1-800-Authors (1-800-288-4677)

ISBN: 978-1-4401-0835-8 (pbk)
ISBN: 978-1-4401-0836-5 (ebk)

Printed in the United States of America

iUniverse rev. date: 1/12/09

PREFACE

It has been reported that in the 1940s a survey listed the top seven discipline problems in public schools:

1) Talking
2) Chewing gum
3) Making noise
4) Running in the halls
5) Getting out of line
6) Wearing improper clothes
7) Not putting paper in the wastebaskets

A more recent survey lists the top seven today:

1) Drug abuse
2) Alcohol abuse
3) Pregnancy
4) Suicide
5) Rape
6) Robbery
7) Assault

As a chemistry teacher, it became clear to me that students must be guided and challenged in today's world. The answer is obviously not drugs used for behavior problems. Students often leave our schools confused, without intellectual satisfaction, which often creates negative attitudes. This discourages them intellectually from entering life and debating societal issues and from utilizing the basic concepts for critical thinking and problem solving.

True understanding of concepts is essential for successful application of knowledge without concept understanding. Under such circumstances, misconceptions about science and God's true nature of the world arise. The fact is ordinary men and women have cured disease, put man on the moon, and placed our society into a new era of communication via the computer. But the fact remains that ordinary men and women became God's instruments to deliver the message of Christ to planet Earth.

Teachers must not only teach their subject area, but also they must be God's instruments to disciple young minds on Godly living and serving humanity through moral instruction. Science offers theories to explain facts through observation and experimentation. Theology explores truth. In this book, I hope to encourage the best problem-solvers, who are driven by an enthusiasm for knowledge and for success in science, to bridge that relationship with the bible for a betterment of our society and to understand the power that Jesus Christ has to correct our lives and the world in which we live.

Acknowledgments

I would like to thank my parents, Millard and Betty, for bringing me up in a Christian home; my wife, Rebecca, and brother, Gary, who encouraged me to write this book; and Pastor Bill Cahill and members of the Clintwood United Methodist Church for giving me the opportunity to demonstrate some of the ideas for *Science in the Pulpit.* I would also like to thank Mitzi Sykes for helping me prepare my book for the publishing company. But most of all, I would like to thank Jesus, who enabled me to write this book relating science and the Bible.

Contents

Chapter 1

—— CONDUCTIVITY ——

And God said, "Let There be light," and there was light.
And God saw the light, that it was good, and God divided
the light from the darkness.
—Genesis 1:3–4

Although we are earthen vessels, we carry in us the glory of God. If our world is going to get the message of God's glory, it must come through us.

We understand this in Colossians 1:27:
To whom God would make known what is the riches of the glory of this mystery among the Gentiles, which is Christ in you, the hope of glory.

2 Corinthians 4:6
For God, who commanded the light to shine out of darkness, hath shined in our hearts to give the light of the knowledge of the glory of God in the face of Jesus Christ.

Let us look at a conductivity apparatus for chemistry and conductivity for life: the Bible. It has been said the Bible is the basic instructions before leaving Earth. In chemistry, you have orderly sequential patterns, primarily positive before negative. In the bible, you have orderly sequential patterns: good triumphs over evil and light before darkness. Light reveals sins.

The conductivity apparatus in chemistry measures the degree of ionization through dissociation. This is seen in the original Bohr model or through quantum mechanics. You can calculate the atomic radii or electron negativity of chlorine or the ionization of sodium. Simply put, sodium has one electron to give away, and chlorine has one electron to accept. As a compound, salt does not produce a current. Only when water is added do the sodium and chlorine ions dissociate. The positive ion is attached to the negative pole while the negative ion is attached to the positive pole.

Demonstration with Conductivity Tester:
1) Take some salt in a beaker and place in the tester. The bulb does not light up.
2) Take another beaker, and place water in the tester. The bulb does not light up.
3) Take the salt and put in the water: the Na^+ and Cl^- are now dissociated into their positive and negative ions, and there is light.

This conductivity can be purchased from Flinn Scientific, Inc., Batavia, Illinois.

In our lives it is the belief that through Christ and through the baptism of water, we are reborn to live a Christian life, and we are really dissociated from the world to let our light shine.

James 4:4
Ye adulterers and adulteresses, know ye not the friendship of the world is enmity with God? Whoever therefore will be a friend of the world is the enemy of God.

You see, we cannot serve both darkness and light.

John 3:19–21
And this is the condemnation, that light is come into the world, and men loved darkness rather than light because their deeds were evil. For everyone that doeth evil hateth the light, neither cometh to the light lest his deeds should be reproved. But he that doeth truth cometh to the light, that his deeds may be manifest that they are wrought in God.

Isaiah 8:20
To the law and to the testimony; if they speak not according to this word, it is because there is not light in them.

2 Corinthians 6:14
Be ye not unequally yoked together with unbelievers, for what fellowship hath righteous with unrighteousness? And what communion hath light with darkness.

Matthew 5:14–16
Ye are the light of the world. A city that is set on a hill cannot be hid. Neither do men light a candle and put it under a bushel but on a candlestick, and it giveth light unto all that are in the house. Let your light so shine before men, that they may see your good works and glorify your Father, which is in Heaven.

Psalms 27:1
The Lord is my light and my salvation; whom shall I fear? The Lord is the strength of my life; of whom shall I be afraid?

John 8:12
Then spake Jesus again unto them, saying, "I am the light of the world. He that followeth me shall not walk in darkness, but shall have the light of life."

Revelation 21:23
And the city had no need of the sun neither of the moon to shine on it, for the glory of God did lighten it, and the lamb is the light thereof.

Just as with our demonstration of sodium and chlorine, if our positive flows toward the negative, eventually the negative will flow toward positive. It is sad to say, our lives are the only bible some people ever read.

In closing, Jesus calls us to be agents of his common grace by commanding us to salt and to light the world. Salt seasons and preserves, and light warms and dispels darkness. We are called to preserve the good in our culture and to make it tasteful. We are to bring light, love, laughter, and morality into society.

Luke 14:34
Salt is good, but if the salt have lost his savour, wherewith shall it be seasoned?

It can be seasoned with the light of God through his son Jesus Christ.

1 John 1:5
God is light, and in him is no darkness at all

We turn to God for help when our foundations are shaking, only to learn that it is God shaking them.

—Charles West

Chapter 2

– Color Demonstration –

Laughing children hold hands while they dance around singing "Ring around the rosy, pocket full of posies, ashes, ashes, we all fall down." Children of the twenty-first century probably know nothing of the tragic history behind this familiar old rhyme. The voices of fourteenth-century children sang the song of rose petals that doctors carried in their pockets, believing the rose fragrance would ward off the Black Plague. The song's ending, "ashes, ashes, all fall down," is in reference to the bodies that were stacked and burned after dying from the plague. This dreaded infectious disease killed one-quarter of Europe's population.

Today, we think them silly for believing that rose petals could stop the Black Plague. In the future, will people look back and think us silly for trying to stop the AIDS virus with the slogan "Safe Sex?" God recorded through Moses the standards and guidelines for avoiding sickness using good hygiene and the rules of isolation with people infected with contagious diseases. Leviticus instructions as recorded in the Bible were used for people to have a long and healthy life.

Read the twentieth chapter of Leviticus to see how old sins can be repackaged for our new age.

Genesis 19:4–8
Lot offered his two daughters to the men of Sodom, but the men wanted his two Angelic visitors. Sodom and Gomorrah are probably the most noted cultures that were destroyed because of their sexual promiscuity.

Many sports stars, TV stars, and movie celebrities who tragically choose to live promiscuous lives send the message "Safe Sex" without a message of abstinence.

The intrinsic voids in our safe sex packages i.e. condoms have some holes to the HIV virus which is 1/10 of a micron in size (four millionths of an inch). The Bible forewarns that the only safe sex is within a wisely chosen marriage.

Ice will melt when heated whether you believe it or not.

Fire will burn your hand whether you believe it or not.

The Earth is not flat whether you believe it or not.

God's word is real whether you believe it or not.

AIDS is not the only factor. Fifty million Americans are infected with genital herpes; one youth contracts syphilis or gonorrhea every 30 seconds in America. Ten million victims of sexually transmitted diseases last year were under twenty-five years of age.

Thirty percent of sexually active teens in America are infected with chlamydia. The risk of these infections increases according to the number of sexual partners one has.

Leviticus chapter 18 and Romans 1:24–32 tell us "God gave unto man and woman vile affections and a reprobate mind."

The Greek word translated Adokimos, meaning debased or reprobate, speaks of something useless. In other words, the mind becomes useless spiritually and morally.

1 Thessalonians 4:2–4
For ye know what commandments we gave you by the Lord Jesus. For this is the will of God, even your sanctification that ye should abstain from fornication: Then every one of you should know how to possess his vessel in sanctification and humor.

How did a few AIDS cases grow into an epidemic? The following example demonstrates a ten-minute epidemic.

Have ten to twenty youth in a group. Each participant will have a container of clear solution to represent body fluids.

Instruct one group to be Sodom and Gomorrah, and instruct the other group to be abstinent.

In each group, there will be a carrier. For this demonstration, lye—sodium hydroxide, colorless in water—will be used to simulate our virus, and no one will know which container has the virus.

In the Sodom and Gomorrah group, use an eye dropper to let number one pour some of his or her solution into number fifteen. Fifteen will drop some of his or her solution into number seven and so on. This is an example of random sharing.

When they have completed the exchanges, add a pH indicator, in this case phenolphthalein. If the color changes to pink, the individual has been infected. This is a good demonstration to show how the person who was initially infected did not have to be with each person directly for the infection to spread. In the abstinent group, only one should have turned purple or pink.

We have an answer for sin, and the cure is found in 2 Chronicles 7:14:
If my people, which are called by my name, shall humble themselves and pray and seek my face and turn from their wicked ways, then will I hear from Heaven and will forgive their sin and will heal their land.

What to do:
Put on safety glasses. The chemical solution you are using can burn. If you get any on yourself, rinse the area immediately with lots of cold water.

What you need:
A container half filled with water for each person: one container in each group should contain a small amount of lye, pH indicator (phenolphthalein), thirty eye droppers, and safety glasses.

CHAPTER 3

——— NEEDLE TRICK ———

*And ye now therefore have sorrow: but I will see you again,
and your heart shall rejoice, and your joy no man taketh
from you.*

—John 16:22

The story is told of a farming community in which most
of the farmers were godly men who gathered to worship
the Lord on Sunday instead of working their fields. One
exception was a farmer who was an atheist. He considered
himself a freethinker and often chided his neighbors,
saying, "Hands that work are better than hands that pray."
Part of his land bordered the church, and he would make
a point of driving his tractor by during worship services.
When one year his land produced more than anyone
else's in the county, he submitted a lengthy letter to the
editor of a local paper, boasting of what a man can do
on his own without God. The editor printed the man's
letter, and added this pithy comment: "God doesn't settle
all his accounts in the month of October."

Author Unknown

How do we find happiness in our present world: riches,
drugs, alcohol, recognition, or multiple relationships?
We find happiness through readjusted mental attitudes

with Jesus Christ. Jesus overcame the impossible. The great tempter, Satan, offered him all the kingdoms of the world to reject his Father. Jesus was not accepted by his fellows. He lived among the oppressed. Freedom was not known. Religion was restrictive. He came from Nazareth, which most people thought nothing good came from there. Jesus was not educated. His followers were ordinary men and women. He suffered rejection and betrayal. He was whipped and finally crucified on the cross. But while on the cross, he said, "Father forgive them for they know not what they do" (Luke 23:34).

To Jesus, problems became possibilities. The most precious possibility came from his death: life goes on beyond death. Our basis for Christianity is Jesus' Resurrection. Jesus proved that he lived by dying. Jesus should make us feel impressed and not depressed. Jesus gave hope, comfort, and mercy.

In Philippians 4:11–13, Paul believed what Jesus had said and done:
Not that I speak in respect of want, for I have learned, in whatever state I am, therewith to be content. I know both how to be abased, and I know how to abound. Everywhere and in all things, I am instructed both to be full and to be hungry, both to abound and to suffer need. I can do all things through Christ, which strengthened me.

In the Sermon on the Mount, Matthew 5:3–12, we read the Beatitudes, or the positive attitudes, which were Jesus' understanding of how God's Kingdom differed from what passed for religion, not only in his time but also in ours. The Random House Dictionary Revised Edition Copyright 1980 defines beatitude in one way as supreme blessedness, exalted happiness.

Blessed are the poor in spirit, for theirs is the Kingdom of Heaven.
Blessed are they that mourn, for they shall be comforted.
Blessed are the meek, for they shall inherit the Earth.
Blessed are they which do hunger and thirst after righteousness, for they shall be filled.
Blessed are the merciful, for they shall obtain mercy.
Blessed are the pure in heart, for they shall see God.
Blessed are the peacemakers, for they shall be called the children of God.
Blessed are they which are persecuted for righteousness' sake, for theirs is the Kingdom of Heaven.
Blessed are ye, when men shall revile you and persecute you and shall say all manner of evil against you falsely, for my sake.
Rejoice, and be exceedingly glad, for great is your reward in Heaven, for so persecuted they the prophets which were before you.

Now we are going to do a demonstration of being pierced. Have you ever seen someone put a 22-inch needle through a balloon without the balloon popping? It can be done.

Step 1
Place a small amount of Vaseline inside the balloon where the needle will enter and exit.

Step 2
Blow up the balloon, and tie it off.
Step 3
Insert the needle through one Vaseline covered end, and continue sliding the needle through until it pierces the other Vaseline covered end.

You can pull the needle completely through the balloon, and the balloon will stay inflated. The Vaseline helps fill the air holes. If you take a pin and stick the balloon where there is no Vaseline, it will pop.

This example illustrates that in life, no matter how we are pierced by sickness, divorce, and problems of all kinds, we can stay inflated through the fullness of Jesus who was pierced for all mankind.

Without Christ we will pop.

Isaiah 53:5
But he was wounded for our transgressions; he was bruised for our iniquities. The chastisement of our peace was upon him, and with his stripes, we are healed.

Jesus knew what he had to do, and he did it. He knew that he had to die an unmerciful death in order to save men.

Living the exalted happiness that we received from Jesus' Sermon on the Mount should make us realize the impact of salvation and how it affects the attitude we have toward life. Jesus wants us in charge of our attitudes regardless of education, money, success, failures, or what others think—regardless of would've, could've, should've.

As the demonstration illustrates, a relationship with Jesus Christ keeps us feeling blessed, or filled with his spirit. Without a relationship with Jesus Christ, we will pop.

Balloon needle kit can be purchased from Flinn Scientific, Inc., catalog No. AP1969, PO Box 219, Batavia, Illinois 60510-0219, Telephone 1-800-452-1261.

CHAPTER 4

——— SUPER BALL ———

If you are going through Hell, keep on going.
—Winston Churchill

Why does God allow the righteous to suffer? Why do some people seem to bounce back and others' faith hold very little patience?

Psalms 119:71
It is good for me that I have been afflicted that I might learn thy statutes.

Romans 8:16–18
"The spirit itself bareth witness with our spirit that we are the children of God. And if children, then heirs; heirs of God, and joint-heirs with Christ; if so be that we suffer with him, that we may be also glorified together. For I reckon that the sufferings of this present time are not worthy to be compared with the glory which shall be revealed in us.

David's suffering was in preparation for the Throne. He was a soldier, but he suffered in the wilderness to learn how to trust God and how not to trust flesh. How, then, do we bounce back from the death of a loved one, sickness, or sorrow, which often seems to be more than we can bear?

Conquering our circumstances is largely dependent upon the spirit with which we face them.

Hebrews 5:8
Though he were a son, yet learned he obedience by the things which he suffered.

When a blacksmith tempers iron, he heats it red hot and then plunges it into ice cold water. He then heats and hammers it unmercifully. Sometimes it gets too brittle and falls apart. This is thrown into a scrap pile. The real iron to the blacksmith remains strong. In life, we cannot always have good times. Sometimes, like the old song "I'm coming up on the rough side of the mountain; I must hold on to God's unchanging hand," God has put the temper of Christ in us by testing us with trials. Let us pray for strength to bounce back from our trials and not fall apart and get placed in a scrap pile. God is making us strong because he is preparing us for his Kingdom privileges.

Today, we will look at a demonstration to show how we can bounce.

Super Ball

Science Concept:
Sodium silicate reacts with ethanol, forming a polymer that has rubber properties.

Materials:
sodium silicate solution (40%)
ethanol

food coloring
stirring rod
100 ml graduated cylinder
400 ml beaker
10 ml graduated cylinder
latex gloves
paper towels

Directions:

1) Measure 20 ml of sodium silicate solution in the 100 ml graduated cylinder.
2) Pour the sodium silicate solution into the 400 ml beaker.
3) Add food coloring, if desired, to the sodium silicate solution.
4) Measure 5 ml of ethanol in the 10 ml graduated cylinder.
5) Add the ethanol to the sodium silicate solution.
6) Stir the solutions quickly as the solid begins to form.
7) When mixture is solid, remove from beaker using latex gloves. If the mixture still has not formed a solid, add 5 ml more of ethanol.
8) Start molding the mixture into a ball, using paper towels to dry it as you work.

Be careful not to mold it too hard as it will crumble.

Explanation:

In this demonstration we concentrated on the element silicon. Silicon is found in sand and is a major element found in computer chips. The liquid solution of sodium silicate is already in the form of a polymer. The silicate alternates atoms of silicon and oxygen. These long chains are called polymers. When the ethanol is added, it bridges and connects the chains by cross-linking them. The analogy of a chain-link fence is a good picture of the idea of chains that are cross linked. That is what the ethanol and the silicate are doing to form this super ball.

Safety:
Use latex gloves to keep hands clean while working with it when it is wet.

Disposal:
If there is any excess of the rubber ball, dispose of it in the garbage.

Reference:
Borgford, C, and Sommerlin, L, Chemical Activities, American Chemical Society, 1988, p. 89.

In closing, we must look at the Twenty-third Psalm and its meaning with certain word relations.

Shepherd	Salvation
Not Want	Satisfaction
Green Pastures	Rest
Still Waters	Refreshment
Soul	Restoration
Righteousness	Guidance
Fear No Evil	Protection
With Me	Company
Table	Provision
Cup	Joy

Good & Mercy   Care
Dwell   Destiny

Praise God for giving his son to die on the cross to save us. He is the reason we can really bounce back. Jesus acted on our behalf to keep us going. He gave an iron-clad, systemized plan of approach, and it is our Christian mission to use our mind, heart, soul, and strength to bounce back and not be unknowable to the world.

John 16:33
These things I have spoken unto you, that in me ye might have peace. In the world ye shall have tribulation, but be of good cheer; I have overcome the world.

CHAPTER 5

PH

Let my sentence come forth from thy presence; Let thine eyes behold the things that are equal.

—Psalm 17:2

In science, the pH of a solution shows the terms of the hydrogen-ion concentration. The pH scale ranges from 0 to 14. Solutions with a pH above 7 are basic, and solutions below 7 are acidic. Neutral solutions have a pH of 7. Being able to determine pH is important for many reasons, including the facts that our stomach utilizes acid for digestion, blood and urine have a certain pH, and any changes to bodily pH can affect one's health. Similarly, different plants require different soil pH to grow and be healthy.

The lower a number falls below 7 on the pH scale, the stronger the acid. The higher the number goes above 7, the stronger the base. Strong acids and strong bases are corrosive.

Acids and bases can be determined using indicators. One good example is litmus paper. Sometimes we have heard people say, "This is the litmus test." Blue litmus paper will turn red in an acid solution. Red litmus paper will turn blue in a basic solution. If you have litmus paper, test some vinegar as well as some baking soda water as a visible demonstration.

In the following demonstration, red cabbage is used to identify an acid and a base.

Materials:
Red Cabbage
Hot Plate
Water 100 ml
Glassware such as one 200ml beaker
Safety Goggles

In one beaker add 5 to 10 ml of vinegar and in the second beaker add 5 to 10 ml household ammonia. You should wear goggles because household ammonia is poisonous.

Preparation:
Combine red cabbage and water in a beaker and bring to a boil on the hot plate. Decant, or pour off, the solution into another beaker.

Results:
Ammonia added to the cabbage water results in the appearance of the color green. Vinegar added to the cabbage water results in the color pink.

So the cabbage juice is an acid base indicator due to the color changes of an acid and base in the cabbage juice. Use a black board, smart board, or a large piece of white poster board. The pH scale looks like this:

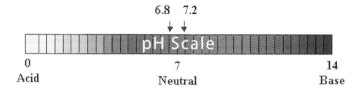

6.8 7.2

pH Scale

0   7   14
Acid   Neutral   Base

In chemistry, equilibrium is symmetry that keeps reaction systems in balance. The Chinese might recognize this balance as yin and yang. Science uses terms such as positive and negative ions. The world might find things out of equilibrium, or balance, as good or evil.

So it is a fact that when we are out of balance it becomes an impediment to our body and our spiritual well-being. In a sense, we become too acidic or too basic, too far to the left or too far to the right. So a body out of balance becomes unsteady from a lack of self-control. It takes a relationship with Jesus to become a person of balance.

So now let's look at the pH scale with Jesus as the center and one true force restoring balance to our lives. When Jesus was hanging on the cross between Heaven and Earth with outstretched arms, he became the balance neutralizing the force pulling us to the corrosive or acidic ends. The cross becomes our pH scale with Jesus at the center of balance.

Seven is an important number in the Bible. Seven expresses completeness through the union of Earth and Heaven.

Seven symbolizes spiritual perfection.

Revelations: 7 Churches
                7 Stars
                7 Spirits
                7 Seals
                7 Trumpets

The number seven is used in Leviticus 23:8, 15–16.

There are 7 feasts in Leviticus

There are 7 Dispensations

1) Innocence
2) Conscience
3) Government
4) Patriarchy
5) Law
6) Grace
7) Millennia Age

Jesus said to forgive seventy times seven.

Genesis 7:2
Noah took the clean beasts into the Ark by sevens.

Genesis 7:10
Seven days after Noah went into the Ark, the flood came.

Leviticus 16:14
On the Day of Atonement, the priest sprinkled blood seven times.

Joshua 6:1–16
Israel took the city of Jericho by marching seven times.

Revelation 5:12
There is a sevenfold praise of the lamb that was slain.

1) Power
2) Riches
3) Wisdom
4) Strength
5) Honor
6) Glory
7) Blessing

Life operates in a cycle of seven:

7 Bones in the neck
7 Bones in the face
7 Bones in the ankle
7 Bones in the head

There are seven notes in the musical scale.

What are our indicators in Life? Do we act sour as an acid or bitter as a base? Are we pulled to the right or left to have corrosive attitudes? Or are we centered through the balance that Jesus Christ brings in our lives?

What should our pH in life be to find the balance in Jesus Christ:

<u>P</u>ray <u>H</u>ard

And if we truly pray hard, we find that it is Jesus who brings balance to us and our unstable world.

CHAPTER 6

——— NYLON ROPE ———

A wise old owl sat in an oak
The more he saw, the less he spoke
The less he spoke, the more he heard
Why can't we be like that wise old bird?
　　　　　　　　　　　　　　—Nursery Rhyme

After we meet Jesus, we must listen to him. Jesus is depending on us to bring others to him. How can we make the word of God refreshing to others and not leave them dry and exhausted?

What a pleasure for Paul to meet Onesiphorus in 2 Timothy 1:16:
The Lord give mercy unto the house of Onesiphorus, for he oft refreshed me and was not ashamed of my chains.

Paul needed a pick-me-up; he needed that extra lift from a brother in fellowship with God. Instead of talking about others, we need to think of others. We should talk about our blessings in Christ. We should have compassion, concern, and a genuine desire to help others. Faith produces spiritual fruit in works that are done with the proper motive of glorifying God. It should be a delight to be in the presence of a refreshing Christian because their life emulates encouragement and blessings.

We see the spirit of Brotherhood and love throughout Romans chapter 16.

Romans 15:30, 32
Now I beseech you, brethren for the Lord Jesus Christ sake, and for the love of the spirit, that ye strive together with me in your prayers to God for me ... that I may come unto you with joy by the will of God and may with you be refreshed.

We, as Christians, should work and pray to agonize against the forces of evil so that we can win the battle for Christ. Something comes out of it when we fellowship with other believers and encourage each other. How refreshing to know that even a ten-minute visit with an old or homebound person can be more effective than twenty-four hours of nursing care.

Paul was asking to pray with him and for him. When David prays, the lions are muzzled. When Nehemiah prays, the king's heart is softened. When the church in Jerusalem prays, Peter is delivered. When Paul and Silas pray, the prison doors are opened. These are just a few illustrations from the bible of how prayer works in lives.

James 5:16
Confess your faults one to another, and pray one for another that ye may be healed. The effectual fervent prayer of a righteous man availeth much.

The Nylon Rope Trick

Procedure for Demonstration

Use rubber gloves and safety goggles and don't let the chemicals touch your skin.

In the science laboratory, make the following:

1) Into a 50 ml beaker, pour first solution made up of 6 grams of hexamethylenediamine. Add 2 grams of sodium hydroxide solution. Then add 2 to 3 drops of red food coloring. OR If using hexamethylenediamine/sodium hydroxide solution, pour 15 ml of solution into a 50 ml beaker. Omit the food coloring.

2) Make a solution of 5 ml adipoyl chloride and 5 ml cyclohexane, or measure 10 ml of adipoyl chloride/hexane solution. Pour this solution down the walls of the beaker (like pouring soda down the side of a glass to reduce the fizz). The two solutions will not mix, and immediately a polymer will form at the liquid-liquid interface.

3) Using a ten-inch wire with a hook at the end, gently free the polymer strings from the walls of the beaker (like taking the batter away from the sides of a mixing bowl).

4) Withdraw the wire with polymer strings attached, and then hook the polymer strings at the center.

5) Gently raise the wire so that the polymer forms continuously, producing a nylon filament that can be drawn many feet.

6) Rinse the filament several times in the pan of water, and lay it on a paper towel to dry.

7) If you want to continue making nylon rope (and who wouldn't?), stir the remainder of the solution with the wire, let it settle, and start again.

8) Dispose of the waste.

If you pour an oil solution into a glass containing water, the point where the oil and water don't mix but perch on top of each other is, in simple terms, called an interface: a common boundary or interconnection between systems.

The previous demonstration is an example of something coming out of a boundary between two solutions. It is called the Nylon Rope trick.

So now we see something come out of the two solutions.

Let us make something come out of our prayers. Let us be refreshing Christians like Onesiphorus. God is so great and good. He is righteous and holy. God is loving and all wise. He is our healer and refuge. God is our joy and peace. At least we can be refreshing Christians and not build resistance in people. Let us not interface between each other with a common boundary but lift each other up to have mutual support and witness.

We need to be like the wise old owl and listen and not misconstrue conversion as an isolated experience to have a solitary religion.

We can only pray to understand that the Christian life is a partnership with Jesus and believers of Him. We can only pray that something will come out of our Christian journey. By being a refreshing Christian, we may bring the decision of accepting Jesus Christ as a personal savior to someone who is lost.

Nylon Rope Experiment can be purchased from Flinn Scientific Inc.,P.O. Box 219, Batavia Illinois 60510-0219, Telephone 1-800-452-1261

CHAPTER 7

────── MOH ──────

From my interpretation of The Steve Miller Band's song "Fly Like an Eagle" it illustrates what it means to help people with hardships. These hardships include feeding people, helping children and housing people.

This is the same advice Jesus tells his disciples. In Deuteronomy 32:4: He is the rock, his work is perfect: for all his ways are judgment: a God of truth and without iniquity, just and right is he.

Our measurement in how we manage the hardships of life for ourselves or our witness to others depends on our relationship with Jesus.

A rock is defined in the Random House College Dictionary as a large mass of stone forming a hill cliff, promontory, or the like. A firm foundation or support: The Lord is my rock.

Identifying the hardness of rocks relies on chemistry using the MOHs test, or measurement of hardness scale. Metaphorically, a rock denotes a foundation that cannot be changed or moved, a way to build our hopes for happiness.

1 Corinthians 10:4
And did all drink the same spiritual drink, for they drank of that spiritual rock that followed them, and that rock was Christ.

In Matthew 16:18, Jesus changed the name of Simon (soft) to Peter (rock) to reveal his character. Peter's confession of faith in Christ is the rock upon which the church is built.

Ephesians 2:20
And are built upon the foundation of the apostles and prophets, Jesus Christ himself being the chief cornerstone. In whom all the building fitly framed together growth unto a holy temple in the Lord. In whom ye also builded together for an habitation of God through the spirit.

Psalms 89:26
He shall cry unto me, thou art my father, my God, and the rock of my salvation.

Today we are going to do a demonstration of how to perform the MOHs Test.

As in testing the hardness of different materials in chemistry, it is helpful to know the hardness of our rock through salvation.

Matthew 7:24
Therefore whosoever hearth these sayings of mine and doeth them, I will liken him unto a wise man, which built his house upon a rock.

How do we solidify ourselves like a rock? Through Jesus: first by confession, then by doing God's work on Earth with responsibility.

Ephesians 5:15–17 and 1 Thessalonians 5:14–18 can be summed up as live life with a due sense of responsibility, not as men who do not know the meaning and purpose of life but as those who do. Make the best use of your time despite all the difficulties of these days. Don't be vague, but firmly grasp what you know to be the will of God.

From the song "Fly Like an Eagle" I think there is a solution that will solidify our life and become a rock to help others and that is through Jesus Christ.

How to Perform the MOHs Test

Identifying rocks and minerals relies heavily on chemistry, but most of us don't carry around a chemistry lab when we're outside, and most of us do not have one to take rocks back to when we come home. So, how do we identify rocks? We gather information about our treasure to narrow down the possibilities. It's helpful to know the hardness of the rock. Rock hounds often use the MOHs test to estimate the hardness of a sample. In this test, you scratch an unknown sample with a material of known hardness. Here's how you perform the test yourself.

Difficulty: Easy

Time required: mere seconds

Here's how:

1) Find a clean surface on the specimen to be tested.

2) Try to scratch the surface with the point of an object of known hardness by pressing it firmly into and across your test specimen. For example, you could try to scratch the surface with the point on a crystal of quartz (hardness of 9), the tip of a steel file (about 7), the point of a piece of glass (about 6), the edge of a penny (3), or a fingernail (2.5). If your 'point' is harder than the test specimen, you should feel it bite into the sample.

3) Examine the sample. Is there an etched line? Use your fingernail to feel for a scratch because sometimes a soft material will leave a mark that looks like a scratch. If the sample is scratched, then it is softer than or equal to your test material. If the unknown was not scratched, it is harder than your tester.

4) If you are unsure of the results of the test, repeat the test using a sharp surface of the known material and a fresh surface of the unknown.

5) Most people don't carry around examples of all ten levels of the MOHs hardness scale, but you probably have a couple of 'points' in your possession. If you can, test your specimen against other points to get a good idea of its hardness. For

example, if you scratch your specimen with glass, you know its hardness is less than 6. If you can't scratch it with a penny, you know its hardness is between 3 and 6. Calcite has a MOHs hardness of 3. Quartz and a penny would scratch it, but a fingernail would not.

Tips:

1) Try to collect examples of as many hardness levels as you can. You can use a fingernail (2.5), penny (3), piece of glass (5.5-6.5), piece of quartz (7), steel file (6.5-7.5), sapphire file (9).

What You Need:

- **Unknown specimen**
- **Objects of known hardness (e.g., coin, fingernail, glass)**

Chapter 8

CO₂

… and then some

*Shortly after a business executive retired, someone
asked him what had been the secret of his success.
He chuckled softly, and then said that it could be
summarized
in three words: "and then some."
He explained that he had learned early in his career
that the top people in any group were those who did
what was expected of them … and then some.
Such people worked diligently, efficiently, faithfully,
… and then some. They were thoughtful and kind to
others
… and then some. They were reliable friends who
could be counted on … and then some. If an emergency
came, they tried to do their share to deal with it … and
then some. In short, they were more than ordinary people,
they tried to be extraordinary.
That is precisely what Jesus expected and still
expects of his followers. When he was teaching his
friends about loving and serving others (Matt.
5:43–48), he included these words: "What more are you
doing than others?" (v.47, NRSV).
Christians do what is required … and then some.*

—Anonymous

It is not success that God rewards but faithfulness in doing his will. Is God pleased with our Christian service? Have we, as believers in Christ, risen faithfully to use opportunities he has given us?

James 1:22
But be ye doers of the word, and not hearers only, deceiving your own selves.

To support each other, we must rise to our responsibility to serve Christ.

Let us look at an example of how to rise up.

Soda water contains carbon dioxide gas, which collects on the surface of irregular objects such as raisins. Drop some raisins in a tall glass or graduated cylinder filled with soda water. The raisins will initially sink to the bottom, but once enough bubbles have collected on the raisins, the bubbles will lift the raisins to the surface where the gas is released into the air. Once this happens, the raisins will sink again. This demonstration is a good example of how our church family and friends can support each other and lift each other up when we stumble or fall.

From start to finish, biblical writers were concerned with the mighty saving and uplifting acts of God. One trait that is outstanding in the lives of Jonah, Ester and Nehemiah was obedience. At first, Jonah disobeyed God and was later lifted out of a whale. The three Hebrews were lifted up, and God kept them safe in the fiery furnace. Ester was lifted up, obeyed God, and helped save her people. Nehemiah was lifted up, obeyed God, and rebuilt the wall of Jerusalem. Jesus had the ultimate experience of being uplifted.

If we rise up and obey God, He will use us, just like in the hymn, "Trust and Obey."

In the book, *Faith Sharing,* by H. Eddie Fox and George E. Morris: Discipleship Resources, Nashville, Tennessee, Copyright 1996; I read this interesting story: A man, while working in the forest, suddenly fell into an abandoned well. He tried to climb the slippery sides of the well but to no avail. Finally, in complete desperation, he sat down in the muck and mire at the bottom of the well and began to pray, "Oh God, please send someone to rescue me from this well." Suddenly, he heard a voice from above. He looked up, and there, silhouetted against the sky, was the face of a man. He cried out to the man above, "Please save me from this well."

The man above heard his plaintive cry and threw a rope down the well with the instruction to fasten the rope about his waist. With the aid of the rescuer above, the man was able to climb the slippery sides of that well, and he was saved! It was such an exhilarating experience of "being saved" that the saved man spent the rest of his life chasing after people and throwing them down wells so he could rescue them.

Let us rise up not like the man from the well. Like the raisins in the soda water, with God's help we can be lifted up for God's work. Sometimes we have to go down to help someone up. Just as God sent forth His Son to save mankind, we must do what John proclaimed in chapter 20, verse 21: Jesus said, "As the Father sent me, so I send you."

CHAPTER 9

──── BALLOON OR EGG ────

A song from Nickleback entitled "If Everyone Cared" seems to explain how people care, love, and swallow their pride.

We all have a purpose in life hopefully to believe in Christ and follow his commandments. The bible is filled with universal truths about God with promises on which we can build our lives.

Our conscience is really our internal warning system. Pain, like guilt, serves a purpose. If you touch a hot stove, you feel pain. If you play with fire, you may get burned. So pain serves a purpose to not touch a hot stove or play with fire. If we do wrong, we feel guilt. If we didn't, we would do wrong over and over. God has created us with a conscience to become moral, responsible beings.

Romans 2:15
They show that in their hearts they know right from wrong, just as the law commands. And they show this by their conscience.

Do we know right from wrong as Christians?

Luke 9:62
No one having put his hand on the plow and looking back is fit for the kingdom of God.

We are constantly exposed to sin to the extent our conscience has a hard time telling right from wrong. The pressure of life causes us to be pulled into sin that our society seems to accept.

Here is a demonstration of pressure and being squeezed into situation it may be hard to get out of.

Isaiah 30:21
If you go the wrong way to the right or to the left, you will hear a voice behind you saying "this is the right way; you should go this way."

Samson experienced great suffering because he gave into temptation, and his conscience was compromised. Sin draws us into a kind of unconsciousness that creates a barrier between us and God. If we do not remove ourselves from the sin that literally draws us in, we will separate ourselves from God.

Sin is like a sinkhole. Once the hole begins, it can get bigger and bigger and swallow up everything in its path.

Satan has attractive temptations to draw us into sin. Like the balloon or egg in the bottle demonstration, we are literally sucked in and become trapped by sin.

The Water-Balloon-in-the-Bottle Trick
(or Egg-in-the-Bottle Trick*)

This uses matches so you **must check** with an adult before you do anything. (Ask them to join in!) Be sure to wear safety goggles.

What you need
- A balloon (ordinary party balloon)
- A wide-mouth bottle (pasta sauce bottles or big juice bottles are great for this, use a glass jar if you can't find a bottle)
- A pair of tongs
- Matches
- A tissue

What to do
- Fill the balloon with water. (Put the balloon onto a tap and fill it until it is slightly bigger than the mouth of the jar or bottle.)
- Holding half of a tissue with tongs, light it with a match.
- Stuff the tissue into the bottle, and quickly put the water balloon on top.
- The balloon should get pushed into the bottle.
- To get the balloon out, tip the bottle and pull on the knot until it pops out.

Why does it work?

As the tissue burns in the bottle, it heats up the air inside. Air expands when you heat it, so the hot air takes up more room than before. You may see it escaping around the water balloon and making the water balloon jump and jiggle.

After the flame goes out, the air in the bottle will cool and contract back to its old size. But the water balloon won't let any more air into the bottle, so the pressure drops inside the bottle. The normal air pressure outside the bottle pushes on the balloon and squeezes it into the bottle.

Notice the water balloon acts as a one-way valve: it lets air out, but it won't let air back in again.

Having Trouble?
Here are the most common mistakes and solutions:
- Don't use too much tissue, it will go out (extinguish itself) before you can get it in through the mouth of the bottle.
- Blow into the bottle between tries; you need new oxygen each time. Once a flame has burned the oxygen inside the bottle, you won't get another flame to survive. But try not to breathe any smoke in because it's not healthy. Instead of blowing, use a hair dryer if you can.
- Maybe your water balloon is just too big, or the mouth of your bottle is just too small.

*The Egg-in-the-Bottle version is the same except you use a hard-boiled egg (peeled) instead of a water balloon. Beware, it's messier and hard to do more than once.

Jesus expected and still expects his followers to love and serve others and not be caught by Satan's snarls. God also knows that the temptations of this world are bad and will result in our harm. Many things can draw us into destructive behavior: addictions, greed, materialism, jealousy, anger, and disease. Our belief in Christ keeps us from being pulled into sin from the pressures of life.

I John 2:16
For everything in the world—the cravings of sinful man, the lust of his eyes, and the boasting of what he has and does—comes not from the father but from the world.

Things of the world are in direct opposition to the things of God. Let us pray not to be pulled into worldly indulging that will put us and God in conflict.

In closing, here is a poem I wrote:

The Caution Light

Upon arrival at the pearly gate,
There was a caution light, and I had to wait.

It was longer than usual, so I asked why,
And the Angel told me as he walked by.

While on Earth, souls were lost,
And they were attributed at your cost.

But I told the Angel I had gone by the rule,
And I had always gone to church and Sunday school.

So how could a man who tried to live right
Be held up at a caution light.

The Christian life has promises to keep,
And Sunday is only one day in a week.

So wherever you go and whatever you say,
Our examples should not cause someone else to go
astray.

Because of the example we set and the way that it
shows,
Means if, at the gate, we will either stop or go.

CHAPTER 10

FLASH PAPER

A story is told about a soldier who was finally coming home after having fought in war. He called his parents: "Mom and Dad, I'm coming home, but I have a favor to ask. I have a friend to bring home with me."

"Sure," they replied, "we'd love to meet him."

"There's something you should know," the son continued, "he was hurt pretty bad in the fighting. He has lost an arm and a leg, he has nowhere else to go, and I want him to live with us."

"I'm sorry to hear that son; maybe we can help him find somewhere else to live."

"No, Mom and Dad, I want him to live with us."

"Son," said the father, "you don't know what you're asking. Someone with such a handicap would be a terrible burden on us. We have our own lives to live, and we can't let something like this interfere with our lives. I think you should just come home and forget about this guy. He'll find a way to live on his own."

At that point, the son hung up the phone. The parents heard nothing more from him. A few days later, they received a call from the city's police department; their son had died after falling from a building. The police believed it was a suicide.

The grief-stricken parents flew to this particular city and were taken to the city morgue to identify the body of their son. They recognized him, but to their horror, they also discovered something they didn't know: their son had only one arm and one leg. The parents, by refusing to help their son's friend, had unknowingly not helped their own son.

—Anonymous

At what point do we have only one quarter, one third, one half of our lives left? The fact is we don't know. Therefore, we don't have time to waste. We should put away our personal desire or any desire that is ahead of God's plan.

Let's do an example of a piece of Flash paper:

Flash paper should be used under adult supervision. FIRE DANGER.

You can purchase flash paper from chemical supply companies, internet, or Dreamland Magic – 8665 W. Flamigo #131-220, Las Vegas, NV, 89147

Light one end and it quickly flames up and is gone in a second.

James 4:14

Where as ye know not what shall be on the morrow. For what is your life? It is even a vapor that appeareth for a little time and then vanisheth away.

If you've wronged someone, tell them you're sorry.

If you've failed to tell someone you love them, tell them you love them.

If you have neglected to tell someone about Jesus, tell them.

Like the flash paper, even in the best of circumstances, life quickly drifts away. Understanding this reality leads us to spend our short life in preparation for what really lasts: eternity with Jesus in Heaven.

CONCLUSION

Genesis 1:11–12

And God said, "Let the Earth bring forth grass, the herb yielding seed, and the fruit tree yielding fruit after his kind, whose seed is in itself, upon the Earth." And it was so. And the Earth brought forth grass, and herb yielding fruit, whose seed was in itself, after his kind, and God saw that it was good.

The universe obeys certain rules to which all things must adhere. These are created by God. These laws are consistent with biblical creation. It is God who has created order on Earth and in the universe. God's logic obeys laws of chemistry that are derived from the laws of physics and mathematics. So according to Genesis chapter 1, God created diverse kinds of life on Earth and made them reproduce their own kind. *The laws of chemistry* explain different properties of elements that bond from atoms into compounds that make up the universe. Even the elements and compounds are not arbitrary in nature. The periodic table logically organizes the elements based on their physical properties. We also have *laws of planetary motion.* There are *laws of physics* that describe the behavior of the universe. Some *laws of physics* are in existence because God wills them to. *The laws of mathematics* are a transcendental truth. This may be because God's nature is logical and mathematical. We even have a *law of logic.* God is logical. God cannot lie or be tempted by sin because this would contradict his perfect nature. Man is created in God's image; therefore, we instinctively know logic so we can reason and know what sin is.

There is uniformity of nature because the laws apply to the future as well as the past. This is the basic assumption of all science. God does not change. In Jeremiah 33:25, God has appointed the ordinances of Heaven and Earth.

All of God's creations should honor him, from the rocks to the trees.

31:8
Nor any tree in the garden of God was like unto him in his beauty.

In closing, here is a poem that I wrote on how even an oak tree can praise God.

I'm Just an Old Oak Tree

Lord, I'm getting old. There's not much time left for this old body. Through the years, I have tried to give food and shelter to those who need it. I have weathered many a storm in my life. But through it all, I have outstretched my arms to Heaven. I have been with you Lord from the beginning. Some of my family members were even with you at Calvary. When I pass on Lord, I hope that part of me will give strength to the uplifting of your church. I am just an old oak tree, but I am one of your treasured creations. Surely all of God's creations should be as fortunate and blessed as me.